PERFECT
PANINI

Mouthwatering recipes for the world's favorite sandwiches

Recipes
JODI LIANO

Photographs
MAREN CARUSO

weldon**owen**

ONE PANINO, TWO PANINI…

Bread and cheese have always been a seductive combination, but the Italians do it best with panini. These "little bread rolls" have become a category of sandwich par excellence, ubiquitous in cafés everywhere. The appeal comes from layering simple, quality ingredients—thinly sliced salami or prosciutto, melting cheeses such as mozzarella or fontina, flavor-packed pestos and spreads—on a hefty slab of focaccia or country bread. Smash it down with conviction on the press, and you've got a hot, delicious creation.

In these pages, you'll find a panino for every craving and occasion. Recipes start with well-loved classics, using the Italian-inspired ingredients most of us associate with panini: savory cured meats, briny olives, grilled eggplant and zucchini, and saucy meatballs. Signature hot sandwiches join in the mix, such as meaty Reubens, spicy ham-and-pickle Cubanos, and cheesy croques. Other recipes riff on lunchtime favorites, featuring grilled chicken, deli ham or turkey, heaps of roasted veggies, even brown-bag PB&J. These sandwiches could be served cold, but with a few tweaks and a quick stint in the press, they transform into warm and toasty panini.

In the second half of the book, see just how versatile and modern panini can be, drawing on special ingredients like grilled salmon or juicy lamb burgers. Slip in fresh flavors with leafy herbs—adding woodsy thyme to mushrooms, or fragrant sage to apples and cheddar. Look for international flavors, such as Spanish manchego cheese or fiery North African harissa. And discover unexpected combinations, such as sweet summer nectarines with Brie, prosciutto with fig jam, roasted pork with pickled onions, and much more.

Panini are effortlessly simple to assemble and cook, as easy to pile on a platter for a picnic or whip up as lunch for one. Whatever you are in the mood for, you'll find countless variations and temptations to savor throughout this book.

THE BEST INGREDIENTS

Perfect panini are easy for anyone to make. Success really depends on using the best-quality ingredients that you can find.

Bread Bread is the foundation of every panino, from the crunchy, toasted exterior to the soft interior. Shop for herbed focaccia, rustic country loaves, fresh baguettes, challah or brioche, and petite rolls. Think about flavor, from tangy sourdough to rye, seeds to whole grains, even walnuts or olives.

Cheese Cheese holds it all together. Choose good semi-firm melting cheeses, which respond well to heat. Aged mozzarella and provolone are the Italian staples; cheddar and Gruyère are solid contenders. But don't overlook spreadable fresh cheeses, luscious triple creams, and boldly flavored blues.

Meats and Seafood Pick up high-quality deli meats like sliced turkey, ham, corned beef, or pastrami, and seek out charcuterie such as mortadella, salami, capicola, or prosciutto. Roasted pork or grilled steak and chicken breasts can all be thinly sliced for stacking. Fry up bacon or sausages, or for a lighter meal, use fresh seafood such as salmon, tuna, prawns, or crabmeat.

Veggies Layer in freshness and crunch with vegetables, from juicy tomatoes and tender greens to slices of roasted eggplant, zucchini, and bell pepper. Tuck a few Italian tricks away in the pantry: jarred roasted peppers, marinated artichoke hearts, spicy peperoncini, and sun-dried tomatoes.

Fruits Swap out vegetables for fruit, especially those that pair well with cheese. Crisp autumn apples and pears love a sharp cheddar or Stilton. Summer stone fruits such as nectarines, peaches, and plums make sweet companions to soft Brie or roasted pork, and pineapple rings caramelize gorgeously on the grill.

Spreads Spreads add another boost of flavor. Try creamy rémoulade, garlicky aioli, briny tapenade, or basil or cilantro pesto. For a sweet note, try fig jam or quince paste, or even a dollop of chutney.

PANINI PERFECTION

You've lined up some quality ingredients, and it's time to stack and press. With these tips and tricks, anyone can craft panini like a maestro.

How to stack Strive for the perfect ratio of bread to filling—not too scant, but not too much of a mouthful. Cheese should go first, then layer meats or veggies in more or less equal parts. Consider flavor and moisture as you go. This is where herbs and spreads come into play, and a judicious slice of tomato here or a swipe of salsa verde there can go a long way.

Go for gooey A good melting cheese (see page 8) and plenty of it is the key to holding a panino together in all of its gooey glory. Cheese should go directly next to the bread, helping to create cohesion with the surrounding ingredients. Two layers, one next to each bread slice, works best. Depending on the spread, you can also layer cheese on one side and spread on the other.

Commit to crispy Once fully stacked, you can press panini just as they are, but the savvy cook will quickly brush some oil or butter on the outside of the bread. A fruity olive oil or creamy butter adds flavor, and helps to toast the bread to a golden finish.

Fire it up Preheat the press, skillet, or grill so that the bread sizzles on impact. Electric presses will automatically heat to a set temperature, and some have a light to indicate when they're ready. If using a frying pan or grill, it's up to you to maintain the right level. Aim for medium to medium-high heat, and be ready to adjust the heat during cooking.

Smash it down Don't be afraid to press! It's what separates panini from their cold counterparts. For the prettiest grill marks, set the sandwiches down at an angle to the ridges, and try to resist nudging or peeking. Halfway through cooking, rotate the sandwiches 90 degrees to create a crosshatched pattern.

TOOLS

Panini are low maintenance. Essentially, all you'll need is something to heat the sandwiches and a method to press them down.

Panini press or electric grill A dedicated panini press is arguably the best tool for the job. These countertop electric devices are specifically designed to grill panini evenly and at just the right temperature. Most feature an adjustable top plate to accommodate all sandwiches, from elegantly thin to jaw-achingly thick. Both panini presses and electric grills often feature ridges to create grill marks, and come in nonstick materials for easy release. An electric grill is slightly more all-purpose, but similar in appearance and use. Intended for searing meats, it can easily accommodate panini as well. Check that you are using the correct temperature settings for sandwiches, and turn halfway through cooking so that the panino is evenly pressed.

Frying pan or grill pan Even without a sandwich press, you probably already have all of the tools you need to create delicious panini at home. Choose a heavy skillet, preferably cast-iron, preheat well, and check the heat regularly for the best results. You just need to improvise a way to press down on the sandwiches. Consider purchasing a panini weight, complete with a handle, that rests on top while the sandwich cooks, or, use a second heavy pan or a brick wrapped in clean aluminum foil to weigh down the sandwich.

Outdoor grills For maximum flavor, fire up the grill. Cooking panini outdoors over gas or charcoal requires a little more attention, but delivers fabulously smoky flavor. Take care not to stoke the heat too high, and experiment with raking the coals to one side. Buttery, cheesy sandwiches should be watched carefully in case of flare-ups, so stand by with tongs if you need to scoot panini over to a cooler safety zone. If you're using a heavy pan, just make sure it's entirely heatproof, including the handle.

Other tools A good serrated knife helps to rip into crusty bread and a pastry brush makes it easy to cover the surface with olive oil or melted butter. A heatproof spatula or tongs are also key for flipping.

CLASSIC PANINI

Three Cheese & Tomato 19

Italian Cheesesteak 20

Muffuletta 23

BLT 24

Reuben 25

Meatball 26

Turkey & Bacon Club 29

Turkey Burger Patty Melt 30

Pimento Cheese 31

Pulled Pork & Slaw 32

Shrimp Po'Boy 35

PB & J 36

Turkey, Brie & Apple 37

Grilled Chicken, Tomato & Mozzarella 38

Egg & Bacon Breakfast Sandwich 41

Roast Beef & Horseradish 42

Crab Melt 43

Cubano 44

Croque Monsieur 47

Roast Turkey & Cranberry 48

Grilled Eggplant & Tapenade 49

Summer Vegetable & Basil 51

It may seem like a no-brainer, but with three types of gooey cheese, juicy tomato slices, and fragrant basil layered between crunchy artisan bread, this sandwich is nothing short of brilliant. Use an herbed fresh goat cheese instead of Boursin if you'd like.

SERVES 2

THREE CHEESE & TOMATO

crusty country-style bread
4 slices, each about
½ inch (12 mm) thick

olive oil
1 tbsp

✛

garlic-and-herb cheese spread such as Boursin
3 tbsp

mozzarella cheese
2 oz (60 g), thinly sliced

provolone cheese
2 oz (60 g), thinly sliced

✛

ripe but firm tomato
4 thin slices

fresh basil leaves
6 large

1. Preheat the sandwich grill. Brush 1 side of each bread slice with oil, then spread the unoiled sides with cheese spread, dividing it evenly. On 2 of the bread slices, layer half of the mozzarella and half of the provolone, then the tomato slices and basil leaves, dividing them evenly. Divide the remaining mozzarella and provolone on top. Place the remaining 2 bread slices on top, cheese sides down, and press gently.

2. Place the panini in the grill, close the top plate, and cook until the bread is golden and toasted and the cheese is melted, 3–5 minutes. Serve.

This Italian version of the famous Philly cheesesteak sandwich is overflowing with thinly sliced skirt steak, garlicky onions and peppers, nutty fontina cheese, and homemade basil pesto.

ITALIAN CHEESESTEAK

small red bell pepper
1, seeded and sliced

yellow onion
1, sliced

long Italian rolls
2, split

garlic
2 cloves, minced

basil pesto
preferably homemade
(page 88), ¼ cup
(2 fl oz/60 ml)

olive oil
3 tbsp

balsamic vinegar
1 tbsp

thin skirt steak
¾ lb (375 g)

fontina cheese
¼ lb (125 g), thinly sliced

1. Heat 2 tbsp of the oil in a frying pan over medium heat. Add the bell pepper, onion, and garlic and cook, stirring, until tender, 5–8 minutes. Remove from the heat, stir in the vinegar, and season with salt and pepper. Set aside.

2. Preheat the sandwich grill. Season the steak with salt and black pepper. Place the steak on the grill, close the top plate, and cook the steak until charred on the outside and medium-rare on the inside, 3–4 minutes. Transfer the steak to a plate, keeping the grill on and wiping the grill plates clean.

3. Brush the crust sides of the rolls with the remaining 1 tbsp oil. Spread the cut sides with pesto. Slice the steak thinly. On the bottom half of each roll, layer the steak, fontina, and onion-pepper mixture, dividing them evenly. Cover with the top halves of the rolls, pesto sides down, and press gently.

4. Place the panini in the grill, close the top plate, and cook until the bread is golden and toasted, the steak is warmed, and the cheese is melted, 3–5 minutes. Serve.

With origins in New Orleans, this hearty deli meat-stuffed wedge is balanced by a bright, vinegary salad of chopped olives, celery, carrots, and cauliflower. If you don't have time to make the olive salad, you can find it at a well-stocked Italian deli.

SERVES 2

MUFFULETTA

round Italian rolls
2, split

olive oil
1 tbsp

+

mortadella
2 oz (60 g), thinly sliced

Genoa salami
2 oz (60 g), thinly sliced

provolone cheese
2 oz (60 g), thinly sliced

capicola or other Italian ham
2 oz (60 g), thinly sliced

mozzarella cheese
2 oz (60 g), thinly sliced

+

Sicilian-style mixed olive salad
preferably homemade (page 91), ½ cup (2½ oz/70 g)

1. Preheat the sandwich grill. Brush the crust sides of the rolls with the oil. On the bottom half of each roll, add the olive salad, dividing it evenly. Layer the mortadella, salami, provolone, capicola, and mozzarella on top, dividing them evenly. Cover with the top halves of the rolls, oiled sides up, and press gently.

2. Place the panini in the grill, close the top plate, and cook until the bread is golden and toasted, the meats are warmed, and the cheese is melted, 3–5 minutes. Serve.

It's hard to improve on a BLT, but by adding triple-cream Saint André cheese and grilling the sandwich in a press, you'll take this classic to a whole new level. Look for ripe but firm summer tomatoes— their sweetness helps to balance the rich, salty flavors.

BLT

pain de mie
4 slices, each about ½ inch
(12 mm) thick

unsalted butter
1 tbsp, room temperature

+

bacon
4 thick slices

Saint André cheese
2 oz (60 g), room
temperature

+

romaine lettuce
4 medium leaves

**ripe but firm
heirloom tomato**
4 thick slices

1. In a frying pan over medium heat, cook the bacon until crisp on both sides, 6–8 minutes. Transfer to paper towels to drain.

2. Preheat the sandwich grill. Spread 1 side of each slice with the butter. On 2 of the bread slices, spread the unbuttered sides with the cheese, dividing it evenly, then layer each with 2 bacon slices, 2 romaine leaves, and 2 tomato slices. Sprinkle the tomatoes with a pinch of salt and pepper. Place a bread slice on top of each, buttered side up, and press gently.

3. Place the panini on the grill, close the top plate, and cook until the bread is golden and toasted and the cheese is melted, 3–4 minutes. Serve.

Piled high with deli staples like corned beef, nutty Swiss cheese, briny sauerkraut, and sweet Russian dressing, this quintessential New York sandwich is not only crave-worthy, but exceedingly addictive. Serve it with crisp dill pickle spears and potato chips.

SERVES 2

REUBEN

rye bread or pumpernickel bread
4 slices, each about ½ inch (12 mm) thick

unsalted butter
1 tbsp, melted

+

Jarlsberg cheese
3 oz (90 g), thinly sliced

corned beef
¼ lb (125 g), thinly sliced

+

Russian dressing
preferably homemade (page 90), about ¼ cup (2 fl oz/60 ml)

fresh sauerkraut
⅓ cup (1½ oz/45 g), drained

1. Preheat the sandwich grill. Brush 1 side of each bread slice with the melted butter, then spread the unbuttered sides with the Russian dressing, dividing it evenly. On 2 of the bread slices, layer half of the cheese, then the corned beef and sauerkraut, dividing them evenly. Divide the remaining cheese on top. Place the remaining 2 bread slices on top, dressing sides down, and press gently.

2. Place the panini in the grill, close the top plate, and cook until the bread is golden and toasted, the corned beef is warmed, and the cheese is melted, 3–5 minutes. Serve.

The succulent meatballs are the stars of this sandwich. If you don't have homemade meatballs, buy them at your favorite Italian deli. Fresh mozzarella is ideal because it melts right into the sauce, making this the messy, drippy delight it absolutely should be.

MEATBALL

ciabatta rolls
2, split

olive oil
1 tbsp

✚

cooked meatballs
preferably homemade
(page 91), 6, halved

fresh mozzarella
¼ lb (125 g), thinly sliced

✚

marinara sauce
preferably homemade
(page 88), about ½ cup
(4 fl oz/125 ml)

chopped peperoncini
¼ cup (1¼ oz/40 g)

1. Preheat the sandwich grill. Brush the crust sides of the rolls with the oil. On the bottom half of each roll, spread about 2 tbsp of marinara, then layer the halved meatballs, peperoncini, and mozzarella, dividing them evenly. Divide the remaining marinara on top. Cover with the top halves of the rolls, oiled sides up, and press gently.

2. Place the panini in the grill, close the top plate, and cook until the bread is golden and toasted, the meatballs are warmed, and the cheese is melted, 4–5 minutes. Serve.

This old-fashioned American sandwich may seem ho-hum, but embellishing it with creamy havarti cheese and then grilling it in a panini press gives it new life. Use the best quality ingredients you can find for the tastiest results.

SERVES 2

TURKEY & BACON CLUB

multigrain bread
4 slices, each about
½ inch (12 mm) thick

olive oil
1 tbsp

+

bacon
4 thick slices

havarti cheese
2 oz (60 g), thinly sliced

smoked turkey
2 oz (60 g), thinly sliced

+

ripe but firm avocado
½, thinly sliced

ripe but firm tomato
4 thin slices

1. In a frying pan over medium heat, cook the bacon until crisp on both sides, 6–8 minutes. Transfer to paper towels to drain.

2. Preheat the sandwich grill. Brush 1 side of each bread slice with the oil. On the unoiled sides of 2 of the bread slices, layer half of the cheese, then the turkey, bacon, avocado, and tomato, dividing them evenly. Divide the remaining cheese on top. Place the remaining 2 bread slices on top, oiled sides up, and press gently.

3. Place the panini in the grill, close the top plate, and cook until the bread is golden and toasted and the cheese is melted, 3–5 minutes. Serve.

SERVES 2

Homemade turkey burgers in crisp panini modernizes the classic patty melt. Opt for dark meat, as it will stay juicier when you cook it. Take your time caramelizing the onions—they're worth the wait.

TURKEY BURGER PATTY MELT

rye bread
4 slices, each about
½ inch (12 mm) thick

olive oil
3 tbsp

+

ground turkey
½ lb (250 g)

minced garlic
½ tsp

large egg
1, beaten

Swiss cheese
2 oz (60 g), thinly sliced

+

yellow onion
1, thinly sliced

mayonnaise
2 tbsp

ketchup
1 tsp

**dill pickle relish
or chopped pickle**
2 tsp

1. Heat 1 tbsp of the oil in a sauté pan over medium heat. Add the onion and cook, stirring, until it begins to brown, 4–5 minutes. Reduce the heat to medium-low and continue cooking until the onion is soft and golden, 25–30 minutes more. Season with salt and pepper and set aside. Meanwhile, stir together the mayonnaise, ketchup, and pickle relish in a small bowl.

2. Preheat the sandwich grill. In a medium bowl, combine the turkey, garlic, egg, and a generous pinch each of salt and pepper. Form the turkey into 2 flat patties and brush both sides of the patties with 1 tbsp of the oil. Place the patties on the grill, close the top plate, and grill until the turkey is cooked through, 7–8 minutes. Transfer the turkey patties to a plate, keeping the grill on and wiping the grill plates clean.

3. Brush 1 side of each bread slice with the remaining oil. On 2 of the slices, spread the unoiled sides with the mayonnaise mixture, dividing it evenly, then layer each with half of the onions, a turkey burger, and half of the cheese. Place the remaining 2 bread slices on top, oiled sides up, and press gently.

4. Place the panini in the grill, close the top plate, and cook until the bread is golden and toasted and the cheese is melted, 3–4 minutes. Serve.

Pimento cheese is a Southern staple, and every mom has her own version. This rendition stands up well to a sandwich grill. Use a roasted red bell pepper in place of the piquillo, if you like.

SERVES 2

PIMENTO CHEESE

sharp cheddar cheese
¼ lb (125 g), coarsely grated

cream cheese
1 oz (30 g), room temperature

pain de mie
4 slices, each about ½-inch (12-mm) thick

olive oil
1 tbsp

+

jarred piquillo pepper
1, drained

mayonnaise
1 tbsp

fresh lemon juice
1 tsp

hot-pepper sauce
1–2 dashes

+

dill pickle
1, thinly sliced

1. In a food processor, add the cheddar, cream cheese, piquillo pepper, mayonnaise, lemon juice, and hot-pepper sauce. Process until combined, taste, and season with salt and black pepper. Transfer to a small bowl. (The pimento cheese can be refrigerated in an airtight container for up to 3 days; bring to room temperature before using.)

2. Preheat the sandwich grill. Brush 1 side of each bread slice with the oil, then spread the unoiled sides with pimento cheese, about 1 tbsp per slice (reserve the remaining for another use). Arrange the pickle slices on 2 of the bread slices, then place the remaining 2 bread slices on top, oiled sides up, and press gently.

3. Place the panini in the grill, close the top plate, and cook until the bread is golden and toasted and the cheese is melted, 3–4 minutes. Serve.

This sandwich is an ideal vehicle for leftover pulled pork. The tangy slaw retains its crunch, cutting the richness of the meat and keeping the flavors balanced. For a saucier panino, serve it with vinegary barbecue sauce for dipping.

PULLED PORK & SLAW

onion rolls
2, split

olive oil
1 tbsp

+

cooked pulled pork
1½ cups (9 oz/280 g),
room temperature

sharp white cheddar
2 oz (60 g), coarsely grated

+

shredded red cabbage
1 cup (3 oz/90 g)

cider vinegar
2 tbsp

honey
1 tsp

celery seeds
1 tsp

1. In a medium bowl, combine the cabbage, vinegar, honey, celery seeds, and a generous pinch each of salt and pepper. Set aside for 30–45 minutes.

2. Preheat the sandwich grill. Brush the crust sides of the rolls with the oil. On the bottom half of each roll, layer half of the pork, a heaping spoonful of the slaw (reserve the remaining slaw for another use), and half of the cheese. Cover with the top halves of the rolls, oiled sides up, and press gently.

3. Place the panini in the grill, close the top plate, and cook until the bread is golden and toasted, the pork is warmed, and the cheese is melted, 3–4 minutes. Serve.

Slathered with creamy rémoulade sauce, heaped with sweet fried shrimp, and topped off with crunchy iceberg lettuce, this traditional New Orleans submarine sandwich is nothing short of divine. To add spice, drizzle it with hot-pepper sauce.

SHRIMP PO'BOY

submarine rolls
2, split

canola oil
1 tbsp

yellow cornmeal
¼ cup (1¼ oz/35 g)

salt
¼ tsp

cayenne pepper
⅛ tsp

medium shrimp
½ lb (250 g)

canola oil for frying

rémoulade sauce
preferably homemade
(page 90), about 4 tbsp

**shredded
iceberg lettuce**
½ cup (½ oz/15 g)

1. Preheat the oven to 200°F (95°C). Stir together the cornmeal, salt, and cayenne on a plate. Peel and devein the shrimp, then place them on the plate, half at a time, and turn to coat with the cornmeal.

2. In a deep frying pan or saucepan, heat 2 inches (5 cm) of oil to 375°F (190°C) on a deep-frying thermometer. Working in 2 batches to avoid crowding, add the shrimp and fry until golden, crisp, and opaque throughout, about 1–2 minutes per batch. Let the oil return to 375°F between batches. Using a slotted spoon, transfer the shrimp to paper towels to drain. If not using immediately, keep warm in a single layer in the oven.

3. Preheat the sandwich grill. Brush both sides of the rolls with the 1 tbsp oil. Open the rolls, put them on the grill, and cook until lightly toasted, about 1 minute. On the bottom half of each roll, spread half of the rémoulade sauce, then layer with the shrimp and shredded lettuce, dividing them evenly. Cover with the top halves of the rolls and press gently.

4. Place the panini back in the grill, close the top plate, and cook until the bread is golden and toasted, about 2–3 minutes. Serve.

Why settle for a boring peanut butter and jelly sandwich when you can craft something remarkable? Toasty cinnamon bread, warm peanut butter, and your favorite fruity jam—try something wild like morello cherry, nectarine, or fig—elevate this to new heights.

PB & J

cinnamon bread
4 slices, each about ½ inch
(12 mm) thick

unsalted butter
1 tbsp, room temperature

**smooth or chunky
natural peanut butter**
¼ cup (2½ oz/75 g)

jam or preserves
2 tbsp

1. Preheat the sandwich grill. Spread 1 side of each bread slice with the butter, then spread the unbuttered sides with the peanut butter, dividing it evenly. On 2 of the bread slices, spread the jam over the peanut butter, dividing it evenly. Place the remaining 2 bread slices on top, peanut butter sides down, and press gently.

2. Place the panini in the grill, close the top plate, and cook until the bread is golden and toasted and the peanut butter is warmed, 2–4 minutes. Serve.

Smoky, tart-sweet, peppery, creamy, crunchy...the ingredients in this simple-yet-sophisticated sandwich come together for an amazing texture, color, and taste combination. A drizzle of walnut oil and a sprinkle of fresh thyme finish it off perfectly.

SERVES 2

TURKEY, BRIE & APPLE

whole-wheat country-style bread
4 slices, each about ½ inch (12 mm) thick

walnut oil or olive oil
2 tbsp

chopped fresh thyme
2 tsp

+

Brie cheese
2 oz (60 g), thinly sliced

smoked turkey
2 oz (60 g), thinly sliced

Granny Smith apple
6 thin slices

+

watercress
½ small bunch, tough stems removed

fresh lemon juice
½ tsp

1. Preheat the sandwich grill. In a small bowl, stir together the oil and thyme. Brush 1 side of each bread slice with half of the thyme oil.

2. On 2 of the bread slices, layer the unoiled sides with half of the Brie, the turkey, apple slices, and watercress, dividing them evenly. Drizzle with the lemon juice and the remaining thyme oil, dividing them evenly, and sprinkle with pepper to taste. Divide the remaining Brie on top. Place the remaining 2 bread slices on top, oiled sides up, and press gently.

3. Place the panini in the grill, close the top plate, and cook until the bread is golden and toasted, the apple and turkey are warmed, and the cheese is melted, 3–5 minutes. Serve.

A lemony marinade on the chicken—which is grilled in the sandwich press—gives this deceptively simple panino a complex layer of flavor. Showcasing fresh basil, ripe tomato slices, and creamy mozzarella, it's perfect for the summer months.

GRILLED CHICKEN, TOMATO & MOZZARELLA

focaccia
2 pieces, each about 4 inches (10 cm) square, halved horizontally

olive oil
1 tbsp

+

skinless, boneless chicken breast halves
2 (about ¼ lb/125 g each), flattened to about ½ inch (12 mm) thick

marinade (page 90)
¼ cup (2 fl oz/60 g)

mozzarella cheese
2 oz (60 g), thinly sliced

+

ripe but firm tomato
4 thin slices

fresh basil leaves
6 large

1. Place the chicken in a dish with all but 1 tbsp of the marinade and turn to coat. Let stand at room temperature for 15 minutes.

2. Preheat the sandwich grill. Remove the chicken from the marinade and discard the marinade. Place the chicken on the grill, close the top plate, and cook until the chicken is opaque throughout, about 5 minutes. Transfer the chicken to a plate, keeping the grill on and wiping the grill plates clean.

3. Brush the crust sides of the focaccia pieces with 1 tbsp oil. Brush the cut sides with the reserved 1 tbsp marinade. On 2 of the focaccia pieces, layer half the cheese, followed by the chicken, tomato slices, and basil leaves, dividing them evenly. Divide the remaining cheese on top. Cover with the remaining 2 focaccia pieces, marinade sides down, and press gently.

4. Place the panini in the grill, close the top plate, and cook until the bread is golden and toasted and the cheese is melted, 3–5 minutes. Serve.

There are many renditions of this hearty morning dish, but this one takes a turn toward the sophisticated with a sprinkle of tarragon. Swap out the English muffin for whole-wheat bread or try it with a drizzle of hot-pepper sauce for added zing.

SERVES 2

EGG & BACON BREAKFAST SANDWICH

English muffins
2, split, or whole-wheat bread, 4 slices, each about ½ inch (12 mm) thick

unsalted butter
2 tbsp, room temperature

+

bacon
4 thick slices

large eggs
2

chopped fresh tarragon
2 tsp

cheddar cheese
2 oz (60 g), thinly sliced

1. In a frying pan over medium heat, cook the bacon until crisp, 6–8 minutes. Transfer to paper towels to drain. Pour off and discard the bacon drippings.

2. In the frying pan, melt 1 tbsp butter. When the butter melts, crack the eggs into the pan. Cook over medium heat until the whites are set but the yolks are still runny, 3–4 minutes. Sprinkle with the tarragon and season with salt and pepper. Flip the eggs and cook until the yolks are softly set, about 30 seconds.

3. Meanwhile, preheat the sandwich grill. Spread both sides of the English muffins with the remaining 1 tbsp butter. Place the muffins, cut sides up, in the grill, close the top plate, and cook until lightly toasted, 1–2 minutes. On the bottom half of each muffin, layer one-fourth of the cheese, 1 egg, and 2 bacon slices. Divide the remaining cheese on top. Cover with the muffin tops, cut sides down, and press gently.

4. Close the top plate and cook until the muffins are golden and toasted and the cheese is melted, 4–5 minutes. Serve.

Tangy horseradish cream and peppery watercress are the ideal partners for extra-tender, rare roast beef. If you have any left over, this is a great way to use it. Sliced tomatoes would also be a welcome, and fresh, addition to this panino.

ROAST BEEF & HORSERADISH

ciabatta rolls
2, split

unsalted butter
1 tbsp, room temperature

+

roast beef
½ lb (250 g), thinly sliced

Parmesan cheese
1 oz (30 g), shaved with a
vegetable peeler

+

mayonnaise
3 tbsp

sour cream
1 tbsp

prepared horseradish
1 tbsp

**chopped
fresh marjoram**
1 tbsp

watercress
1 small bunch,
tough stems removed

1. In a small bowl, stir together the mayonnaise, sour cream, horseradish, and marjoram. Let stand at room temperature for 10 minutes. (The mayonnaise mixture can be refrigerated in an airtight container for up to 6 hours; bring to room temperature before using.)

2. Preheat the sandwich grill. Spread the crust sides of the rolls with the butter, then spread the cut sides with the mayonnaise mixture, dividing it evenly. On the bottom half of each roll, arrange half of the roast beef and season with salt and pepper. Divide the cheese and the watercress on top. Cover with the top halves of the rolls, butter sides up, and press gently.

3. Place the panini in the grill, close the top plate, and cook until the bread is golden and toasted, the meat is warmed, and the watercress is barely wilted, 3–5 minutes. Serve.

Lemony crab salad is stuffed into New England-style buns, then topped with plenty of melted cheese in this hybrid of two East Coast classics: a lobster roll and Chesapeake Bay-style crabmeat. Find Old Bay seasoning in the spice section of most markets.

CRAB MELT

mayonnaise
¼ cup (2 fl oz/60 ml)

thinly sliced
green onion
3 tbsp

hot dog buns
2, preferably
New England-cut

fresh lemon juice
2 tsp

 grated lemon zest
½ tsp

unsalted butter
1 tbsp, melted

Old Bay seasoning
1 tsp

fresh lump crabmeat
½ lb (250 g)

cheddar cheese
2 oz (60 g), coarsely grated

1. In a small bowl, stir together the mayonnaise, green onion, lemon juice and zest, and Old Bay seasoning. Gently stir in the crabmeat, taking care not to break it up too much.

2. Preheat the sandwich grill. Open the hot dog buns flat and brush both sides with the melted butter. Place the buns, cut sides up, in the grill, close the top plate, and cook until lightly toasted, 2–3 minutes. Leave the buns in the grill and heap the crab salad into them, dividing it evenly, then sprinkle with cheese. Lower the top to within ½ inch (12 mm) of the cheese and hold until melted, 30–40 seconds. Serve.

Layered with roasted pork, ham, melted cheese, and pickles, this is the most beloved sandwich of the Cuban communities in Tampa and Miami. Here, cilantro is added to update this classic combination but you can omit it if you want to be authentic.

CUBANO

long Cuban rolls
or submarine rolls
2, split

unsalted butter
1 tbsp, room temperature

✦

provolone cheese
or Swiss cheese
3 oz (90 g), thinly sliced

roasted pork
2 oz (60 g), thinly sliced

Black Forest ham
2 oz (60 g), thinly sliced

✦

Dijon mustard
1 tbsp

chopped fresh cilantro
1 tbsp (optional)

dill pickle
1, thinly sliced

1. Preheat the sandwich grill. Spread the crust sides of the rolls with the butter, then spread the cut sides with the mustard and sprinkle with cilantro, if using. On the bottom half of each roll, layer one-fourth of the cheese and half of the pork, ham, and pickle slices. Divide the remaining cheese on top. Cover with the top halves of the rolls, mustard sides down, and press gently.

2. Place the panini in the grill, close the top plate, and cook until the bread is golden and toasted, the meats are warmed, and the cheese is melted, 3–5 minutes. Serve.

This gooey panino is not for the faint of heart. With layers of thinly sliced ham, Gruyère cheese, Dijon mustard, and a flavorful homemade cheese sauce, all tucked between grilled country-style bread, it's the ultimate in decadence.

SERVES 2

CROQUE MONSIEUR

French bread or other firm, white country-style bread
4 slices, each about ½ inch (12 mm) thick

unsalted butter
1 tbsp, melted

+

Gruyère cheese
¼ lb (125 g), thinly sliced

Black Forest ham
3 oz (90 g), thinly sliced

+

Dijon mustard
2 tsp

cheese sauce (page 88)
¼ cup (2 fl oz/60 ml)

chopped fresh chives
2 tsp

1. Preheat the sandwich grill. Brush 1 side of each bread slice with the butter. Spread the unbuttered sides with the mustard and the cheese sauce, dividing them evenly. On 2 of the bread slices, layer half of the Gruyère cheese, then the ham and the chives, dividing them evenly. Divide the remaining cheese on top. Place the remaining 2 bread slices on top, cheese sauce sides down, and press gently.

2. Place the panini in the grill, close the top plate, and cook until the bread is golden and toasted, the cheese sauce is warmed, and the Gruyère cheese is melted, 3–5 minutes. Serve.

This flavorful sandwich is like having Thanksgiving dinner stuffed between two slices of bread. Dense pumpernickel pairs nicely with roasted turkey, cranberries, and sage. Make this panino anytime fresh cranberries are available, but frozen can be substituted.

ROAST TURKEY & CRANBERRY

pumpernickel bread
4 slices, each about
½ inch (12 mm) thick

olive oil
1 tbsp

+

fresh cranberries
½ cup (2 oz/60 g)

fresh orange juice
2 tbsp

sugar
3 tbsp

roast turkey
6 oz (185 g), thinly sliced

+

mayonnaise
3 tbsp

Dijon mustard
1 tbsp

chopped fresh sage
1 tbsp

1. In a small saucepan, combine the cranberries, orange juice, and sugar. Bring to a boil over medium heat, stirring to dissolve the sugar. Reduce heat to medium-low and simmer until the berries have popped and the sauce is slightly thickened, 7–9 minutes. Let cool slightly.

2. Preheat the sandwich grill. In a small bowl, stir together the mayonnaise, mustard, and sage. Brush 1 side of each bread slice with oil, then spread the unoiled sides with the mayonnaise mixture, dividing it evenly. On 2 of the bread slices, arrange the turkey, dividing it evenly, and season with salt and pepper. Spoon the cranberry compote over the turkey, dividing it evenly. Place the remaining 2 bread slices on top, mayonnaise sides down, and press gently.

3. Place the panini in the grill, close the top plate, and cook until the bread is golden and toasted and the meat is warmed, 2–3 minutes. Serve.

While cooking eggplant on the sandwich press makes things easy, to get a smokier essence, cook it outside on a charcoal grill. Tapenade, an olive spread, is easy to make at home, but also readily available jarred in Italian markets and most grocery stores.

SERVES 2

GRILLED EGGPLANT & TAPENADE

ciabatta rolls
2, split

olive oil
2 tbsp

garlic
1 clove, minced

+

eggplant
1 small, trimmed and
sliced lengthwise

mozzarella cheese
3 oz (90 g), thinly sliced

+

tapenade
preferably homemade
(page 90), 4 tbsp

ripe but firm tomato
4 thin slices

1. Preheat the sandwich grill. In a small bowl, stir together the oil and garlic. Brush both sides of the eggplant slices with half of the garlic oil, then season with salt and pepper. Place the eggplant in the grill, close the top plate, and cook until the eggplant is tender and lightly charred, 3–5 minutes. Transfer to a plate, keeping the grill on and wiping the grill plates clean. (The eggplant can be grilled up to 3 hours ahead and kept at room temperature; or refrigerate for up to 24 hours and bring to room temperature before using.)

2. Brush the crust sides of the rolls with the remaining garlic oil, then spread the cut sides of the rolls with the tapenade, dividing it evenly. On the bottom half of each roll, layer one-fourth of the cheese, half of the eggplant, and 2 tomato slices. Divide the remaining cheese on top. Cover with the top halves of the rolls, tapenade sides down, and press gently.

3. Place the panini in the grill, close the top plate, and cook until the bread is golden and toasted, the eggplant is warmed, and the cheese is melted, 3–5 minutes. Serve.

Grilling fresh summer vegetables in a sandwich press caramelizes their natural sugars, rendering them succulent and delicious. And even better, it's quick and easy. Slice all of the vegetables into an even thickness so they will cook at the same rate.

SERVES 2

SUMMER VEGETABLE & BASIL

small French baguette
1, split and halved

olive oil
2 tbsp

garlic
1 clove, minced

✦

small yellow or red bell pepper
1, seeded and cut into 6 wedges

small zucchini
1, thinly sliced on the diagonal

small red onion
½, thinly sliced

✦

Parmesan cheese
2 oz (60 g), shaved with a vegetable peeler

fresh basil leaves
8 large

1. Preheat the sandwich grill. In a small bowl, stir together the oil and garlic. Brush both sides of the bell pepper, zucchini, and onion with about half of the garlic oil. Season with salt and pepper. Place the vegetables in the grill, close the top plate, and cook until just tender and lightly charred, 3–5 minutes. Transfer to a plate. Keep the sandwich grill on.

2. Brush the crust sides of the baguette with the remaining garlic oil. On the bottom half of each baguette, layer one-fourth of the Parmesan, 2 basil leaves, and half of the vegetables. Divide the remaining Parmesan and basil leaves on top. Cover with the top halves of the baguette, oiled sides up, and press gently.

3. Place the panini in the grill, close the top plate, and cook until the bread is golden and toasted, the vegetables are warmed, and the cheese is melted, 3–5 minutes. Serve.

MODERN PANINI

Roast Pork, Bacon & Pickled Onions 54

Nectarine, Arugula & Brie 57

Creamy Mushroom & Thyme 58

Zucchini, Feta & Tapenade 59

Roasted Peppers, Goat Cheese & Salsa Verde 60

Jalapeño Popper 63

Apple, Cheddar & Sage 64

Chicken Saltimbocca 65

Lamb, Feta & Harissa Burger 66

Sausage, Fontina & Broccolini Pesto 69

Buffalo Chicken 70

Chorizo Torta 71

Hawaiian 72

Tuna Niçoise 75

Asparagus, Sun-Dried Tomato & Chèvre 76

Prosciutto, Gorgonzola & Fig 77

Caramelized Onion & Smoked Gouda 78

Grilled Salmon & Herbed Cream Cheese 81

Roasted Pork, Provolone & Broccoli Rabe 82

Mushroom, Spinach & Tarragon 83

Marinated Artichoke, Spinach & Parmesan 84

Caribbean Chicken 86

Manchego & Quince 87

With roast pork, crispy bacon, and piquant pepper jack cheese, this panino is downright decadent. Don't be intimidated by the quick-pickled onions—just a few minutes of prep time transforms ordinary red onions into a delightfully tangy garnish.

ROAST PORK, BACON & PICKLED ONIONS

challah rolls or pain de mie rolls
2, split

olive oil
1 tbsp

+

bacon
4 thick slices

pepper jack cheese
2 oz (60 g), thinly sliced

roast pork
¼ lb (125 g), thinly sliced

+

chopped fresh cilantro
1 tbsp

mayonnaise
1 tbsp

pickled onions
preferably homemade (page 90), about ¼ cup (1 oz/30 g)

1. In a frying pan over medium heat, cook the bacon until crisp on both sides, 6–8 minutes. Transfer to paper towels to drain.

2. Preheat the sandwich grill. In a small bowl, mix together the cilantro and mayonnaise. Brush the crust sides of the rolls with the oil, then spread the cut sides of the rolls with the mayonnaise. On the bottom half of each roll, layer one-fourth of the cheese, then the pork, bacon slices, and pickled onions, dividing them evenly. Divide the remaining cheese on top. Cover with the top halves of the rolls, mayonnaise sides down, and press gently.

3. Place the panini in the grill, close the top plate, and cook until the pork is warmed and the cheese is melted, 3–4 minutes. Serve.

Sweet nectarines, accented with honey and freshly ground black pepper, may seem like an unusual combination. But once you try it, you'll be reaching for all kinds of stone fruit. Plums, apricots, or peaches would all work in this summery sandwich.

NECTARINE, ARUGULA & BRIE

levain bread
4 slices, each about
½ inch (12 mm) thick

olive oil
1 tbsp

Brie cheese
2 oz (60 g), room
temperature

**ripe but firm
nectarine**
1, thinly sliced

honey
1 tbsp

baby arugula leaves
½ cup (½ oz/15 g)

1. Preheat the sandwich grill. Brush 1 side of each bread slice with oil, then spread the unoiled sides with the Brie, dividing it evenly. On 2 of the bread slices, layer the nectarine, dividing it evenly. Sprinkle the nectarine with a pinch of salt and a generous pinch of pepper, then drizzle with the honey and top with the arugula. Place the remaining 2 bread slices on top, oiled sides up, and press gently.

2. Place the panini in the grill, close the top plate, and cook until the bread is golden and toasted, the cheese is melted, and the arugula is barely wilted, 3–4 minutes. Serve.

Rich and full of big flavor, this meatless sandwich is ideal for dinner. Choose any mushrooms you like—cremini, portobello, or oyster all work well, and a combination is even better. The watercress lends a peppery punch to the creamy mushroom filling.

CREAMY MUSHROOM & THYME

whole-wheat country-style bread
4 slices, each about
½ inch (12 mm) thick

unsalted butter
2 tbsp, room temperature

olive oil
2 tbsp

+

minced shallots
1 tbsp

mixed mushrooms
½ lb (250 g), thinly sliced

chopped fresh thyme
½ tsp

crème fraîche
2 tbsp

+

watercress leaves
½ cup (½ oz/15 g)

Parmesan cheese
1 oz (30 g), freshly grated

1. Heat 1 tbsp butter and 1 tbsp oil in a sauté pan over medium heat. When the butter has melted, add the shallots with a pinch of salt and cook, stirring occasionally, until softened, 3–4 minutes. Add the mushrooms, thyme, and a pinch each of salt and pepper, and cook, stirring occasionally, until the mushrooms have released their liquid and that liquid has evaporated, 5–6 minutes more. Remove the pan from the heat and stir in the crème fraîche. (The mushroom mixture can be refrigerated in an airtight container for up to 24 hours; bring to room temperature before using.)

2. Preheat the sandwich grill. Brush 1 side of each bread slice with the remaining 1 tbsp oil, then spread the unoiled sides with the remaining 1 tbsp butter. On 2 of the bread slices, layer the mushroom mixture, the watercress, and the Parmesan, dividing them evenly. Place the remaining 2 slices of bread on top, oiled sides up, and press gently.

3. Place the panini in the grill, close the top plate, and cook until the bread is golden and toasted, the mushrooms are warmed, and the watercress is barely wilted, 3–4 minutes. Serve.

The summer farmers' market is the inspiration for this panino. The zucchini and crookneck squash are sliced paper-thin and quickly marinated, giving the sandwich a nice texture. Look for good-quality tapenade at most markets or, better yet, make it yourself.

SERVES 2

ZUCCHINI, FETA & TAPENADE

Pugliese bread
4 slices, each about
½ inch (12 mm) thick

olive oil
2 tbsp

+

**chopped fresh
Italian parsley**
1 tbsp

red wine vinegar
1 tsp

green zucchini
1 small, thinly sliced
lengthwise

**yellow
crookneck squash**
1 small, thinly sliced
lengthwise

+

feta cheese
2 oz (60 g), crumbled

tapenade
preferably homemade
(page 90), 2 tbsp

1. Preheat the sandwich grill. In a large bowl, stir together 1 tbsp oil, the parsley, vinegar, and a pinch each of salt and pepper. Add the zucchini and squash and toss. Let stand at room temperature for 5 minutes.

2. Brush 1 side of each bread slice with the remaining 1 tbsp oil. On 2 of the bread slices, spread the unoiled sides with the tapenade, then layer with the squash mixture and the feta cheese, dividing them evenly. Place the remaining 2 bread slices on top, oiled sides up, and press gently.

3. Place the panini in the grill, close the top plate, and cook until the bread is golden and toasted, the zucchini and squash are just softened, and the cheese is melted, 4–5 minutes. Serve.

Piquillo peppers have a bit more kick than bell peppers. You'll find them roasted in jars, usually packed in olive oil. Paired with the piquant salsa verde, they give this sandwich a distinctive bite that is mellowed by the creamy goat cheese.

ROASTED PEPPERS, GOAT CHEESE & SALSA VERDE

levain bread
4 slices, each about
½ inch (12 mm) thick

olive oil
1 tbsp

+

soft goat cheese
2 oz (60 g), room
temperature

**roasted
piquillo peppers**
4, drained and sliced
open lengthwise

+

**salsa verde
(page 89)**
2 tbsp

1. Brush 1 side of each bread slice with the olive oil. On 2 of the bread slices, spread the unoiled sides with the goat cheese, then layer with the peppers, dividing them evenly. Drizzle with the salsa verde. Place the remaining 2 bread slices on top, oiled sides up, and press gently.

2. Place the panini in the grill, close the top plate, and cook until the bread is golden and toasted and the cheese is melted, 3–4 minutes. Serve.

This unusual sandwich is a fun twist on the bar food favorite, jalapeño poppers. Here, the jalapeño chiles are grilled, not fried, and then paired with crisp bacon, cream cheese, and jack. A drizzle of sweet chile sauce puts this panino over the top.

JALAPEÑO POPPER

bacon
4 thick slices

crusty country-style bread
4 slices, each about ½ inch (12 mm) thick

unsalted butter
1 tbsp, melted

+

fresh jalapeño chiles
2 small

olive oil
1 tbsp

jack cheese
2 oz (60 g), thinly sliced

+

cream cheese
2 oz (60 g), room temperature

Thai sweet chile sauce
2 tbsp

1. In a frying pan over medium heat, cook the bacon until crisp on both sides, 6–8 minutes. Transfer to paper towels to drain.

2. Preheat the sandwich grill. Brush the jalapeños with oil. Place the jalapeños in the grill, close the top plate, and cook until the jalapeños are tender and grill marked, 5–7 minutes. Transfer the jalapeños to a plate, keeping the grill on and wiping the grill plates clean. Let the jalapeños cool slightly, remove and discard the stems and seeds, and slice the jalapeños.

3. Brush 1 side of each bread slice with the butter. On the unbuttered sides of 2 of the bread slices, spread the cream cheese, then the chile sauce, dividing them evenly. Layer with the bacon slices, jalapeño slices, and the jack cheese, dividing them evenly. Place the remaining 2 bread slices on top, buttered sides up, and press gently.

4. Place the panini in the grill, close the top plate, and cook until the bread is golden and toasted and the cheese is melted, 3–5 minutes. Serve.

This delightful sandwich is bursting with the essence of autumn: crisp tart apple slices, cheddar cheese, fresh sage, and toasty walnuts. A swipe of apple butter gives it just the right amount of sweetness. Try it for breakfast!

APPLE, CHEDDAR & SAGE

walnut bread
4 slices, each about ½ inch
(12 mm) thick

walnut oil or olive oil
1 tbsp

+

cheddar cheese
3 oz (90 g), thinly sliced

Granny Smith apple
6 thin slices

+

apple butter
2 tbsp

chopped fresh sage
1 tbsp

1. Preheat the sandwich grill. Brush 1 side of each bread slice with oil. On 2 of the bread slices, spread the unoiled sides with the apple butter, half the cheese, and the apple slices, dividing them evenly. Sprinkle the apple slices with sage and divide the remaining cheese on top. Place the remaining 2 bread slices on top, oiled sides up, and press gently.

2. Place the panini in the grill, close the top plate, and cook until the bread is golden and toasted, the apple is just softened, and the cheese is melted, 3–5 minutes. Serve.

This sandwich transports you to Italy. The combination of the roast chicken, fontina cheese, prosciutto, and sage guarantees every bite bursts with flavor. Store-bought rotisserie chicken works well. Use dark meat if you can; the sandwich will be juicier.

SERVES 2

CHICKEN SALTIMBOCCA

focaccia bread
2 pieces, each about
4 inches (10 cm) square,
halved horizontally

olive oil
1 tbsp

shredded roast chicken
1 cup (6 oz/185 g)

prosciutto
2 oz (60 g) coarsely chopped,
plus 2 thin slices

dried sage
1 tsp

fontina cheese
3 oz (90 g), coarsely grated

1. In a bowl, combine the chicken, chopped prosciutto, sage, and cheese.

2. Preheat the sandwich grill. Brush the crust sides of the focaccia pieces with oil. On 2 of the focaccia pieces, layer the chicken mixture and the prosciutto slices, dividing them evenly. Cover with the remaining 2 focaccia pieces, oiled sides up, and press gently.

3. Place the panini in the grill, close the top plate, and cook until the bread is golden and toasted, the chicken is warmed, and the cheese is melted, 3–4 minutes. Serve.

Harissa is a spicy chile paste used in North African cooking that can be found in most well-stocked markets. For this panino, try to find a thick, burger bun–sized pita. Once these panini come off the grill, carefully open them up and drizzle the yogurt inside.

LAMB, FETA & HARISSA BURGER

individual-sized pita breads or ciabatta rolls
2, split

olive oil
1½ tbsp

+

ground lamb
½ lb (250 g)

ground cumin
½ tsp

cayenne pepper
pinch

harissa paste
2 tbsp

feta cheese
2 oz (60 g), crumbled

+

baby arugula leaves
½ cup (½ oz/15 g)

plain Greek-style yogurt
¼ cup (2 oz/60 g)

1. Preheat the sandwich grill. In a medium bowl, combine the lamb, cumin, cayenne, harissa paste, and a generous pinch each of salt and black pepper. Form the lamb into 2 flat patties. Place half of the feta in the center of each patty, wrap the meat around the cheese, then flatten the patty to enclose the cheese. Brush the patties on both sides with ½ tbsp oil. Place the patties on the grill, close the top plate, and cook until the patties are medium-rare, 5–6 minutes. Transfer the patties to a plate, keeping the grill on and wiping the grill plates clean.

2. Brush the outside of the pitas with the remaining 1 tbsp oil. Slide a lamb burger and half of the arugula into each pita and press gently.

3. Place the panini in the grill, close the top plate, and cook until the pitas are toasted and the arugula is barely wilted, 3–4 minutes. Remove the panini from the grill, drizzle the yogurt inside, and serve.

Broccolini, a relative to broccoli, is tender and mild in flavor. Puréed in pesto, its slight bitterness pairs well with spicy sausages. This is a filling sandwich, so a simple salad is all you need to make it a meal.

SAUSAGE, FONTINA & BROCCOLINI PESTO

ciabatta rolls
2, split

olive oil
1 tbsp

+

spicy Italian sausages
2, split lengthwise

fontina cheese
2 oz (60 g), coarsely grated

+

broccolini pesto (page 89)
about ¼ cup
(2 fl oz/60 ml)

1. Preheat the sandwich grill. Place the sausages, cut side down, on the grill, close the top plate, and grill until the sausages are cooked through, 4–5 minutes. Transfer the sausages to a plate, keeping the grill on and wiping the grill plates clean.

2. Brush the crust sides of the rolls with 1 tbsp olive oil, then spread the cut sides with pesto (reserve any remaining pesto for another use). On the bottom half of each roll, layer with 2 sausage halves and half of the fontina cheese. Cover with the top halves of the rolls, pesto sides down, and press gently.

3. Place the panini in the grill, close the top plate, and cook until the bread is golden and toasted and the cheese is melted, 3–4 minutes. Serve.

This is an indulgent sandwich based on the famed wings—buttery, saucy, and spicy at the same time. The trick to getting that distinctive Buffalo quality is to toss the warm chicken in the sauce right away. Dip your sandwich in the extra sauce if you dare.

BUFFALO CHICKEN

Pugliese bread
4 slices, each about ½ inch (12 mm) thick

unsalted butter
2 tbsp, room temperature

garlic powder
1 tsp

chopped fresh Italian parsley
1 tsp

chopped fresh chives
1 tsp

skinless, boneless chicken breast halves
2 (¼ lb/125 g each), flattened to ½ inch (12 mm) thick

olive oil
1 tbsp

hot sauce, such as Frank's Red Hot
¼ cup (2 fl oz/60 ml)

unsalted butter
1 tbsp, melted

pepper jack cheese
2 oz (60 g), thinly sliced

1. Preheat the sandwich grill. Brush both sides of the chicken with oil and sprinkle with a generous pinch each of salt and pepper. Place the chicken on the grill, close the top plate, and cook until the chicken is opaque throughout, about 5 minutes. Immediately transfer the chicken to a large bowl and add the hot sauce and melted butter. Let stand at room temperature for 15 minutes. Keep the grill on and wipe the grill plates clean.

2. In a bowl, stir together the room-temperature butter, garlic powder, parsley, chives, and a pinch each of salt and pepper. Spread both sides of each bread slice with the flavored butter. Remove the chicken breasts from the bowl, and place them on 2 of the bread slices. Top with the pepper jack cheese, dividing it evenly. Place the remaining 2 bread slices on top and press gently.

3. Place the panini in the grill, close the top plate, and cook until the bread is golden and toasted and the cheese is melted, 3-4 minutes. Serve.

Imagine all of your favorite taco ingredients pressed between a crunchy roll and you've got a torta. This version has a serious kick with the combination of chorizo, chipotle, and jalapeños. Be sure to buy Mexican chorizo, which is an uncooked sausage.

SERVES 2

CHORIZO TORTA

Mexican chorizo
¼ lb (125 g), crumbled

bolillo rolls
2, split

olive oil
1 tbsp

canned black beans
¼ cup (1 ⅔ oz/50 g), drained

chipotle chile in adobo
1, minced, with 1 tsp
adobo sauce reserved

queso fresco
2 oz (60 g), crumbled

minced pickled jalapeños
2 tbsp

ripe but firm avocado
1, thinly sliced

1. In a saucepan over medium heat, cook the chorizo, stirring occasionally, until fully cooked and lightly browned, about 5 minutes. Transfer to paper towels to drain.

2. Preheat the sandwich grill. In a medium bowl, combine the black beans, chipotle chile, and the adobo sauce, mashing the beans to form a coarse paste. Brush the crust sides of the rolls with the oil. On the bottom half of each roll, spread the black bean paste, and layer with the chorizo, jalapeños, avocado, and queso fresco, dividing them evenly. Cover with the top halves of the rolls, oiled sides up, and press gently.

3. Place the panini in the grill, close the top plate, and cook until the bread is golden and toasted, the bean paste is warmed, and the cheese is melted, 3–4 minutes. Serve.

Ham and pineapple are an iconic sweet-and-salty pair. Grilling the pineapple rings makes all the difference in this panino. The fruit caramelizes slightly, which helps the savory qualities in both the ham and the mustard really shine.

HAWAIIAN

Hawaiian bread
4 slices, each about
½ inch (12 mm) thick

olive oil
1 tbsp

+

smoked ham
4 oz (125 g), thinly sliced

jack cheese
2 oz (60 g), coarsely grated

+

fresh pineapple
4 rings, each ½ inch (12 mm)
thick, cores removed

canola oil
1 tbsp

whole-grain mustard
2 tbsp

1. Preheat the sandwich grill. Brush both sides of the pineapple rings with the canola oil and sprinkle with salt and pepper. Place the pineapple on the grill, close the top plate, and cook until the pineapple rings are grill marked, 3–4 minutes. Transfer the pineapple to a plate, keeping the grill on and wiping the grill plates clean.

2. Brush 1 side of each bread slice with the olive oil, then spread the unoiled sides with mustard, dividing it evenly. On 2 of the bread slices, layer the pineapple rings, ham, and cheese, dividing them evenly. Place the remaining 2 bread slices on top, oiled sides up, and press gently.

3. Place the panini in the grill, close the top plate, and cook until the bread is golden and toasted and the cheese is melted, 4–5 minutes. Serve.

This might just be the ultimate tuna sandwich. Inspired by the classic salad, Mediterranean ingredients infuse this panino with tasty texture. It's even better if assembled an hour ahead.

TUNA NIÇOISE

French rolls
2, split

+

olive oil-packed tuna
6-oz (185-g) can, drained,
with 1 tbsp oil reserved

minced fennel bulb
3 tbsp

chopped Niçoise olives
2 tbsp

capers
2 tsp

fresh lemon juice
2 tsp

mayonnaise
3 tbsp

chopped fresh basil
1 tbsp

+

ripe but firm tomato
4 thin slices

red onion
4 thin slices

baby arugula leaves
½ cup (½ oz/15 g)

1. In a bowl, toss together the tuna, fennel, olives, and capers. Add the lemon juice, mayonnaise, and basil and stir to blend. Season with salt and pepper.

2. On the bottom half of each roll, spread half of the tuna mixture, then layer each with half of the tomato, onion, and arugula. Cover with the top halves of the rolls. Wrap the panini tightly in aluminum foil and let stand at room temperature for 15 minutes. (The panini can be refrigerated for up to 1 hour; bring to room temperature before grilling.)

3. Preheat the sandwich grill. Unwrap the panini and brush the crust sides with the reserved oil. Place the panini in the grill, close the top plate, and cook until the bread is golden and toasted, 3–5 minutes. Serve.

Earthy asparagus and fresh spring herbs hold up nicely alongside the sweet, concentrated flavor of sun-dried tomatoes and balsamic vinegar in this panino. Add a thick layer of tangy goat cheese, and the results are memorable.

ASPARAGUS, SUN-DRIED TOMATO & CHÈVRE

white or whole-wheat French rolls
2, split

+

asparagus spears
¼ lb (125 g)

olive oil–packed sun-dried tomatoes
¼ cup (2 oz/60 g), drained and sliced, with 1 tbsp oil reserved

fresh goat cheese
3 oz (90 g), room temperature

+

balsamic vinegar
2 tsp

chopped fresh chives
2 tbsp

chopped fresh thyme
1 tbsp

1. Bring a medium pot of salted water to a boil. Add the asparagus to the boiling water. Cook until tender-crisp, about 3 minutes. Drain the asparagus, rinse under cold water, and then drain again. Pat the asparagus dry.

2. Preheat the sandwich grill. Brush the crust sides of the rolls with the reserved sun-dried tomato oil. Spread the cut sides of the roll with the goat cheese, then sprinkle with the vinegar, chives, and thyme, dividing them evenly. On the bottom half of each baguette, layer the asparagus and the sun-dried tomatoes, dividing them evenly. Cover with the top halves of the rolls, cheese sides down, and press gently.

3. Place the panini in the grill, close the top plate, and cook until the bread is golden and toasted, the asparagus is warmed, and the cheese is melted, 3–5 minutes. Serve.

The salty-sweet ingredients that make up this sandwich could easily be found on a cheese platter. The walnut bread is outstanding but a crusty olive loaf would be delicious, too. Look for fig jam in well-stocked supermarkets.

SERVES 2

PROSCIUTTO, GORGONZOLA & FIG

walnut bread or levain
4 slices, each about
½ inch (12 mm) thick

+

olive oil
1 tbsp

prosciutto
2 oz (60 g), thinly sliced

Gorgonzola cheese
3 tbsp, crumbled

+

fig jam
¼ cup (2 ½ oz/75 g)

I. Heat the olive oil in a frying pan over high heat. Add the prosciutto and cook, turning once or twice, until the edges begin to crisp and curl, 1–2 minutes. Transfer to paper towels to drain. Reserve the oil in the frying pan.

2. Preheat the sandwich grill. Brush 1 side of each bread slice with the oil in the frying pan, then spread the unoiled sides with the jam, dividing it evenly. On 2 of the bread slices, layer the prosciutto and Gorgonzola, dividing them evenly. Place the remaining 2 bread slices on top, jam sides down, and press gently.

3. Place the panini in the grill, close the top plate, and cook until the bread is golden and toasted and the cheese is melted, 3–5 minutes. Serve.

The onions are the secret to this sandwich. To truly caramelize them, be patient—drawing the natural sugars out of the onions takes low heat and time. With the addition of smoky Gouda cheese, this luxurious combination is worth the wait.

CARAMELIZED ONION & SMOKED GOUDA

large yellow onion
1, thinly sliced

brown sugar
1 tsp

levain bread
4 slices, each about ½ inch
(12 mm) thick

balsamic vinegar
1 tsp

olive oil
2 tbsp

smoked Gouda
2 oz (60 g), coarsely grated

1. Heat 1 tbsp oil in a sauté pan over medium heat. Add the onion and cook, stirring, until it begins to brown, 4–5 minutes. Reduce the heat to medium-low and continue cooking until the onion is very soft and golden, 25–30 minutes more. Stir in the brown sugar and balsamic and cook 5 minutes more. Set the onions aside.

2. Preheat the sandwich grill. Brush 1 side of each bread slice with the remaining 1 tbsp oil. On 2 of the bread slices, layer the unoiled sides with half of the Gouda and the onions, dividing them evenly. Divide the remaining Gouda on top. Place the remaining 2 bread slices on top, oiled sides up, and press gently.

3. Place the panini in the grill, close the top plate, and cook until the bread is golden and toasted and the cheese is melted, 3–4 minutes. Serve.

Homemade herbed cream cheese is infinitely better than store-bought versions. This recipe calls for chives, parsley, and tarragon, but use any herbs you like. Look for a crusty sourdough loaf; it will hold up well with the grilled salmon.

GRILLED SALMON & HERBED CREAM CHEESE

sourdough bread
4 slices, each about ½-inch (12 mm) thick

olive oil
2 tbsp

+

salmon fillets
2 (about 5 oz/155 g each), skinned and flattened to about ½ inch (12 mm) thick

+

herbed cream cheese
(page 88)

baby arugula leaves
½ cup (½ oz/15 g)

---

1. Preheat the sandwich grill. Season the salmon fillets with salt and pepper. Drizzle both sides with 1 tbsp oil. Place the salmon on the grill, close the top plate, and cook until the salmon is opaque throughout, 3–5 minutes. Transfer the salmon to a plate, keeping the grill on and wiping the grill plates clean.

2. Brush 1 side of each bread slice with the remaining 1 tbsp oil, then spread the unoiled sides with the herbed cream cheese, dividing it evenly. On 2 of the bread slices, layer the salmon fillets and arugula, dividing them evenly. Place the remaining 2 bread slices on top, oiled sides up, and press gently.

3. Place the panini in the grill, close the top plate, and cook until the bread is golden and toasted, the cheese is melted, and the arugula is barely wilted. Serve.

This Italian sandwich is a classic in Philadelphia. Broccoli rabe is slightly bitter but once it's blanched and quickly sautéed in garlic, it becomes the star of this combination. The roast pork can be homemade or procured from your favorite deli counter.

ROASTED PORK, PROVOLONE & BROCCOLI RABE

ciabatta rolls
2, split

olive oil
2 tbsp

+

roast pork
¼ lb (125 g), thinly sliced

provolone cheese
2 oz (60 g), thinly sliced

+

broccoli rabe
¼ lb (125 g), roughly chopped

minced garlic
½ tsp

red pepper flakes
½ tsp

1. Bring a medium pot of salted water to a boil. Add the broccoli rabe and cook until tender-crisp, 3–4 minutes. Drain, transfer to a bowl of ice water until cool, drain again, then pat dry. Heat 1 tbsp oil in a sauté pan over medium heat. Add the garlic and red pepper flakes and cook, stirring, for 30 seconds. Add the broccoli rabe and cook, stirring, until it is nicely coated with the garlic and oil. Season with salt and black pepper and set aside.

2. Preheat the sandwich grill. Brush the crust sides of the rolls with the remaining 1 tbsp oil. On the bottom half of each roll, layer the pork, broccoli rabe, and cheese, dividing them evenly. Cover with the top halves of the rolls, oiled sides up, and press gently.

3. Place the panini in the grill, close the top plate, and cook until the bread is golden and toasted, the pork is warmed, and the cheese is melted, 3–4 minutes. Serve.

Whether you choose a mixture of wild chanterelles and oyster mushrooms or use cultivated button and cremini mushrooms, you'll have a sandwich with flair. Cognac and fresh herbs enhance the earthiness of the mushrooms and spinach.

SERVES 2

MUSHROOM, SPINACH & TARRAGON

minced shallots
2 tbsp

crusty country-style bread
4 slices, each about ½ inch (12 mm) thick

mixed mushrooms
¼ lb (125 g), thinly sliced

Cognac
2 tbsp

baby spinach leaves
1 cup (1 oz/30 g)

unsalted butter
2½ tbsp, room temperature

chopped fresh tarragon
2 tsp

fontina cheese
3 oz (90 g), thinly sliced

1. Melt 1½ tbsp butter in a sauté pan over medium-high heat. Add the shallots with a pinch of salt and cook, stirring, until softened, 3–4 minutes. Add the mushrooms and a pinch of salt and cook, stirring, until the mushrooms have released their liquid, 5–8 minutes more. Stir in the Cognac and tarragon, and season with salt and pepper. Cook, stirring, for 1 minute more. Let cool slightly.

2. Preheat the sandwich grill. Spread 1 side of each bread slice with the remaining 1 tbsp butter. On 2 of the bread slices, layer the unbuttered sides with half of the cheese, the mushrooms, and the spinach, dividing them evenly. Divide the remaining cheese on top. Place the remaining 2 bread slices on top, buttered sides up, and press gently.

3. Place the panini in the grill, close the top plate, and cook until the bread is golden and toasted, the spinach is barely wilted, and the cheese is melted, 3–5 minutes. Serve.

Who doesn't love old-fashioned spinach-and-artichoke dip? This panini takes the best parts of that dip and transforms them into a crunchy sandwich. Try to find artichoke hearts that are simply marinated—too many seasonings can overwhelm the filling.

MARINATED ARTICHOKE, SPINACH & PARMESAN

white country-style or sourdough bread
4 slices, each about ½ inch (12 mm) thick

olive oil
1 tbsp

+

mayonnaise
1 tbsp

freshly grated Parmesan cheese
2 tbsp

cream cheese
2 oz (60 g), room temperature

hot-pepper sauce
2–3 dashes

marinated artichoke hearts
½ cup (3 oz/90 g), drained well and chopped

+

baby spinach leaves
¼ cup (¼ oz/7 g)

1. In a bowl, combine the mayonnaise, Parmesan, cream cheese, hot-pepper sauce, and a pinch each of salt and pepper. Stir in the artichoke hearts.

2. Preheat the sandwich grill. Brush 1 side of each bread slice with the oil. On 2 of the bread slices, spread the unoiled sides with the artichoke mixture and top with the spinach, dividing them evenly. Place the remaining 2 bread slices on top, oiled sides up, and press gently.

3. Place the panini in the grill, close the top plate, and cook until the bread is golden and toasted, the artichoke mixture is warmed, and the spinach is barely wilted, 3–4 minutes. Serve.

Homemade cilantro pesto, sweet tropical mango, and spicy jerk seasoning give this panino layers of flavor and a Caribbean-style twist. Substitute shredded cooked pork, beef, or even grilled shrimp for the chicken.

CARIBBEAN CHICKEN

Cuban rolls 2, split		shredded cooked chicken 1 cup (6 oz/185 g)		cilantro pesto (page 89) ¼ cup (2 fl oz/60 ml)
olive oil 1 tbsp	+	mayonnaise 2 tbsp	+	fresh mango 6 thin slices
ground allspice ¼ tsp		Caribbean jerk sauce 2 tsp		red onion 4 thin slices

1. Preheat the sandwich grill. In a bowl, combine the chicken, mayonnaise, and jerk sauce. In a small bowl, stir together the olive oil and allspice. Brush the crust sides of the rolls with the seasoned oil, then spread the cut sides with the pesto, dividing it evenly. On the bottom half of each roll, spoon half of the chicken mixture, then layer with 3 mango slices and 2 onion slices. Cover with the top halves of the rolls, pesto sides down, and press gently.

2. Place the panini in the grill, close the top plate, and cook until the bread is golden and toasted and the chicken and mango are warmed, 3–5 minutes. Serve.

Membrillo, or quince paste, is a staple at Spain's tapas bars. The tangy-sweet marmalade is often paired with manchego cheese, creating an ideal salty-sweet balance. The quince paste will be piping hot when this sandwich comes out of the press, so use care.

MANCHEGO & QUINCE

levain bread
4 slices, each about
½ inch (12 mm) thick

unsalted butter
1 tbsp, room temperature

+

quince paste
¼ cup (2½ oz/75 g)

manchego cheese
2 oz (60 g), coarsely grated

+

baby arugula leaves
½ cup (½ oz/15 g)

1. Preheat the sandwich grill. Spread 1 side of each bread slice with the butter, then spread the unbuttered sides with the quince paste, dividing it evenly. On 2 of the bread slices, layer the arugula, a pinch of salt, and the manchego, dividing them evenly. Place the remaining 2 slices of bread on top, buttered sides up, and press gently.

2. Place the panini in the grill, close the top plate, and cook until the bread is golden and toasted and the cheese is melted, 3–5 minutes. Serve.

BASIC RECIPES

MARINARA SAUCE

olive oil, 1 tbsp

garlic, 1 clove, peeled

chopped tomatoes, one 14-oz (440-g) can

Heat the olive oil and garlic in a medium saucepan over medium heat just until the garlic is fragrant, 2–3 minutes. Add the tomatoes and a generous pinch each of salt and pepper and reduce the heat to medium-low. Cook, stirring occasionally, until the sauce reduces and thickens, about 20 minutes.

Purée the sauce using an immersion or traditional blender. (The marinara sauce can be refrigerated in an airtight container for up to 2 days; bring to room temperature before using.)

CHEESE SAUCE

unsalted butter, 2 tbsp

all-purpose flour, 2 tbsp

Dijon mustard, 1 tsp

grated nutmeg, ¼ tsp

whole milk, 1 cup (8 fl oz/250 ml)

Gruyère cheese, ¼ cup (1 oz/30 g) shredded

Melt the butter in a small saucepan over medium heat. Add the flour and cook, whisking, for 1 minute, until a smooth paste forms. Stir in the mustard, nutmeg, and salt and pepper to taste, then slowly whisk in the milk. Cook, whisking, until the sauce comes to a boil and thickens, about 2 minutes. Remove the pan from the heat and stir in the cheese until melted. Cover and keep warm until ready to use.

HERBED CREAM CHEESE

cream cheese, 2 oz (60 g), room temperature

chopped fresh chives, 1 tbsp

chopped fresh Italian parsley, 1 tbsp

capers, 1 tbsp

chopped fresh tarragon, 1 tsp

grated lemon zest, 1 tsp

In a small bowl, combine the cream cheese, chives, parsley, capers, tarragon, lemon zest, and a pinch each of salt and pepper. (The herbed cream cheese can be refrigerated in an airtight container for up to 2 days.)

BASIL PESTO

pine nuts, ¼ cup (1¼ oz/35 g)

fresh basil leaves, 2 cups (2 oz/60 g) tightly packed

garlic, 2 cloves, chopped

olive oil, 3 tbsp

Parmesan cheese, 1 oz (30 g), freshly grated

Place the pine nuts in a small, dry skillet over medium-low heat. Cook, stirring constantly, until lightly toasted, 3–5 minutes; watch carefully, as they can burn quickly. Transfer to a plate to cool.

In a food processor, add the toasted pine nuts and basil and process until combined. Add the garlic and pulse to finely chop. With the motor running, slowly pour in the olive oil and process to a smooth purée. Add the cheese and pulse to blend. Season with salt and pepper. (The basil pesto can be refrigerated in an airtight container for up to 2 days or in the freezer for up to 1 month; bring to room temperature before using.)

CILANTRO PESTO

pine nuts, ¼ cup (1¼ oz/35 g)

small jalapeño, 1, seeded and chopped

fresh cilantro leaves, 1½ cups (1½ oz/45 g)

green onion, ¼ cup (¾ oz/20 g) chopped

garlic, 2 cloves, chopped

salt, ½ tsp

olive oil, ½ cup (4 fl oz/125 ml)

jack cheese, 1 oz (30 g), coarsely grated

fresh lime juice, 2 tsp

Place the pine nuts in a small, dry skillet over medium-low heat. Cook, stirring constantly, until lightly toasted, 3–5 minutes; watch carefully, as they can burn quickly. Transfer immediately to a plate to cool.

In a food processor, add the toasted pine nuts, jalapeño, cilantro, green onion, garlic, and salt and process until combined. With the motor running, slowly pour in the olive oil and process to a smooth purée. Add the cheese and lime juice and pulse to blend. (The cilantro pesto can be refrigerated in an airtight container for up to 2 days or in the freezer for up to 1 month; bring to room temperature before using.)

BROCCOLINI PESTO

broccolini, ½ lb (250 g), tough ends removed

toasted pine nuts, 2 tbsp

fresh basil leaves, ¼ cup (¼ oz/7 g)

olive oil, ¼ cup (2 fl oz/60 ml)

freshly grated Parmesan cheese, 2 tbsp

Bring a pot of salted water to a boil. Chop the broccolini and add it to the pot. Cook until tender-crisp, 2–3 minutes. Drain, transfer to

a bowl of ice water until cool, drain again, then pat dry. In a food processor, add the broccolini, pine nuts, basil, and ¼ cup (2 fl oz/ 60 ml) olive oil. Pulse until blended. Transfer to a bowl, stir in the cheese, and season with salt and pepper. (The pesto can be refrigerated in an airtight container for up to 24 hours; bring to room temperature before using.)

SALSA VERDE

fresh Italian parsley leaves, ¼ cup (¼ oz/7 g)

fresh mint leaves, 2 tbsp

olive oil, 3 tbsp, plus more as needed

capers, 2 tsp

minced garlic, 1 tsp

red wine vinegar, ½ tsp

anchovy fillet, 1 small, minced

In a blender or food processor, add the parsley, mint, olive oil, capers, garlic, vinegar, and anchovy and pulse until combined. Transfer the mixture to a bowl and season with salt and pepper. (The salsa verde can be refrigerated in an airtight container for up to 24 hours; bring to room temperature before using.)

TAPENADE

Niçoise or Kalamata olives, ½ cup
   (2½ oz/75 g), pitted
capers, 1 tbsp
anchovy fillet, 1, minced
minced garlic, 1 tsp
grated lemon zest, 1 tsp
freshly ground pepper, ½ tsp
olive oil, 2–3 tbsp

In a food processor, combine the olives, capers, anchovy, garlic, lemon zest, pepper, and 2 tbsp olive oil. Pulse to form a course puree, adding more oil if needed for spreadability. (The tapenade can be refrigerated in an airtight container for up to 5 days; bring to room temperature before using.)

RÉMOULADE SAUCE

mayonnaise, ½ cup (4 fl oz/125 ml)
tomato paste, 2 tsp
Dijon mustard, 2 tsp
white wine vinegar, 1 tsp
chopped fresh chives, 1 tbsp
chopped cornichons, 1 tbsp
chopped fresh Italian parsley, 1 tbsp
chopped fresh tarragon, 2 tsp
coarsely chopped capers, 1 tsp

In a small bowl, stir together the mayonnaise, tomato paste, mustard, and vinegar. Stir in the chives, cornichons, parsley, tarragon, and capers. Let stand at room temperature for 15 minutes to allow the flavors to blend. (The rémoulade sauce can be refrigerated in an airtight container for up to 2 days.)

RUSSIAN DRESSING

mayonnaise, ¼ cup (2 fl oz/60 ml)
ketchup, 2 tsp
prepared horseradish, ¼ tsp
minced yellow onion, ½ tsp
Worcestershire sauce, ¼ tsp
chopped fresh Italian parsley, 2 tsp

In a small bowl, stir together the mayonnaise, ketchup, horseradish, onion, Worcestershire sauce, and parsley. (The Russian dressing can be refrigerated in an airtight container for up to 2 days.)

MARINADE

olive oil, 3 tbsp
fresh lemon juice, 1 tbsp
grated lemon zest, 1 tsp
garlic, 1 clove, minced
salt, ¼ tsp
red pepper flakes, ⅛ tsp

In a bowl, whisk together the olive oil, lemon juice and zest, garlic, salt, and red pepper flakes. (The marinade can be refrigerated in an airtight container for up to 2 days.)

PICKLED ONIONS

small red onion, 1, thinly sliced
rice vinegar, ¼ cup (2 fl oz/60 ml)
sugar, 1 tsp
salt, ½ tsp

Place the sliced onion in a colander in the sink, pour boiling water over it, and drain.

In a saucepan over medium heat, stir together the rice vinegar, sugar, and salt and bring to a boil. Add the onion, return to a boil, and cook until tender, about 5 minutes. Set aside to cool completely. (The pickled onions can be refrigerated in an airtight container for up to 5 days; bring to room temperature before using.)

SICILIAN-STYLE MIXED OLIVE SALAD

pimento-stuffed green olives, ¾ cup 5 oz/155 g), drained and coarsely chopped

mild pickled giardiniera (cauliflower, carrots, and cocktail onions), ⅓ cup (2 oz/60 g), drained and finely chopped

small celery rib, 1, finely chopped

garlic, 1 clove, minced

chopped fresh oregano, 1 tsp

olive oil, 3 tbsp

In a bowl, combine the olives, giardiniera, celery, garlic, and oregano. Add the oil and toss until combined. Let stand at room temperature for 30 minutes to allow the flavors to blend. (The olive salad can be refrigerated in an airtight container for up to 2 days; bring to room temperature before using.)

MEATBALLS

olive oil, 2 tsp, plus more for baking sheet

minced yellow onion, ¼ cup (1½ oz/45 g)

coarse fresh bread crumbs, ½ cup (1 oz/30 g)

whole milk, ¼ cup (2 fl oz/60 ml)

large egg, 1, beaten

chopped fresh Italian parsley, 2 tsp

dried oregano, ½ tsp

ground beef, ½ lb (250 g)

ground pork, ½ lb (250 g)

Preheat the oven to 400°F (200°C). Lightly oil a rimmed baking sheet. Heat the 2 tsp oil in a small frying pan over medium heat. Add the onion and cook, stirring occasionally, until softened, about 4 minutes. Transfer to a large bowl and let cool slightly.

In a small bowl, soak the bread crumbs in the milk for 5 minutes. Squeeze the milk out of the bread crumbs and discard the milk. Add the soaked bread crumbs, egg, parsley, oregano, ½ tsp salt, and a pinch of pepper to the onion mixture and mix well. Add the ground beef and pork and mix just until combined.

Using wet hands, shape the mixture into 6 meatballs, and arrange on the prepared baking sheet. Bake until the tops are browned, about 15 minutes. Turn the meatballs and bake until they are cooked through, about 10 minutes more. (The meatballs can be refrigerated in an airtight container for up to 2 days; bring to room temperature before using.)

INDEX

weldon**owen**

Jackson Street, Suite 200, San Francisco, CA 94111
Telephone: 415 291 0100 Fax: 415 291 8841
www.weldonowen.com

Weldon Owen is a division of
BONNIER

WELDON OWEN, INC.

CEO and President Terry Newell
VP, Sales and Marketing Amy Kaneko
Director of Finance Mark Perrigo

VP and Publisher Hannah Rahill
Executive Editor Kim Laidlaw

Creative Director Emma Boys
Senior Art Director Kara Church

Production Director Chris Hemesath
Production Manager Michelle Duggan

Photographer Maren Caruso
Food Stylist Kevin Crafts
Prop Stylist Ethel Brennan

PERFECT PANINI

Conceived and produced by Weldon Owen, Inc.
Copyright © 2013 Weldon Owen, Inc.

All rights reserved, including the right of
reproduction in whole or in part in any form.

Printed and bound by 1010 Printing, Ltd. in China

First printed in 2013
10 9 8 7 6 5 4 3 2 1

Library of Congress Control Number:
2012948240

ISBN-13: 978-1-61628-543-2
ISBN-10: 1-61628-543-5

Weldon Owen wishes to thank the following people for their generous support
in producing this book: Amanda Anselmino, Jane Tunks Demel, Becky Duffett,
Sean Franzen, Cody Gantz, Anna Grace, Jennifer Hale, Eve Lynch,
Hope Menghermann, and Elizabeth Parson.